MEDUSA

VS.

HEL

Disclaimer:

The creatures in this book are not real. They are from myths. They are fun to imagine. Read the 45th Parallel Press series Gods and Goddesses of the Ancient World to learn more about them.

Published in the United States of America by Cherry Lake Publishing
Ann Arbor, Michigan
www.cherrylakepublishing.com

Reading Adviser: Marla Conn, MS, Ed., Literacy specialist, Read-Ability Inc.
Book Designer: Melinda Millward

Photo Credits: © delcarmat/Shutterstock.com, back cover, 10, 29; © Irina Alexandrovna/Shutterstock.com, cover, 5; © FlexDreams/Shutterstock.com, cover, 5; © camilkuo/Shutterstock.com, 6; © GhostKnife/Shutterstock.com, 9; © Yuri Schmidt/Shutterstock.com, 11; © Ivy Close Images/agefotostock.com, 12; © Nejron Photo/Shutterstock.com, 15; © Patrimonio Designs /Dreamstime.com, 16; © Shelli Jensen/Shutterstock.com, 19; © GraphicsRF/Shutterstock.com, 19, 20; © vectortatu/Shutterstock.com, 20; © Paz Spinelli/Alamy Stock Photo, 21; © Ng Ho Wing/Shutterstock.com, 23; © Kozyreva Elena/Shutterstock.com, 24; © Ana Blazic Pavlovic/Shutterstock.com, 25; © Africa Studio/Shutterstock.com, 25; © Stasia04/Dreamstime.com, 27

Graphic Element Credits: © studiostoks/Shutterstock.com, back cover, multiple interior pages; © infostocker/Shutterstock.com, back cover, multiple interior pages; © mxbfilms/Shutterstock.com, front cover; © MF production/Shutterstock.com, front cover, multiple interior pages; © AldanNi/Shutterstock.com, front cover, multiple interior pages; © Andrii Symonenko/Shutterstock.com, front cover, multiple interior pages; © acidmit/Shutterstock.com, front cover, multiple interior pages; © manop/Shutterstock.com, multiple interior pages; © Lina Kalina/Shutterstock.com, multiple interior pages; © mejorana/Shutterstock.com, multiple interior pages; © NoraVector/Shutterstock.com, multiple interior pages; © Smirnov Viacheslav/Shutterstock.com, multiple interior pages; © Piotr Urakau/Shutterstock.com, multiple interior pages; © IMOGI graphics/Shutterstock.com, multiple interior pages; © jirawat phueksriphan/Shutterstock.com, multiple interior pages

45th Parallel Press is an imprint of Cherry Lake Publishing.

Library of Congress Cataloging-in-Publication Data

Names: Loh-Hagan, Virginia, author.
Title: Medusa vs. Hel / by Virginia Loh-Hagan.
Other titles: Medusa versus Hel
Description: Ann Arbor, Michigan : Cherry Lake Publishing, 2020. | Series: Battle Royale: lethal warriors |
    Includes bibliographical references and index.
Identifiers: LCCN 2019032871 (print) | LCCN 2019032872 (ebook) | ISBN 9781534159327 (hardcover) |
    ISBN 9781534161627 (paperback) | ISBN 9781534160477 (pdf) | ISBN 9781534162778 (ebook)
Subjects: LCSH: Medusa (Greek mythology)—Juvenile literature. | Hel (Norse deity)—Juvenile literature.
Classification: LCC BL820.M38 L64 2020 (print) | LCC BL820.M38 (ebook) | DDC 292.2/16—dc23
LC record available at https://lccn.loc.gov/2019032871
LC ebook record available at https://lccn.loc.gov/2019032872

Printed in the United States of America
Corporate Graphics

About the Author

Dr. Virginia Loh-Hagan is an author, university professor, and former classroom teacher. She has written 45th Parallel Press books about Norse and Greek gods and goddesses. She also has a Sleeping Bear Press book coming out in 2020 about Norse mythology. She lives in San Diego with her very tall husband and very naughty dogs. To learn more about her, visit www.virginialoh.com.

Table of Contents

Introduction

Imagine a battle between Medusa and Hel. Who would win? Who would lose?

Enter the world of *Battle Royale: Lethal* **Warriors**! Warriors are fighters. This is a fight to the death! The last team standing is the **victor**! Victors are winners. They get to live.

Opponents are fighters who compete against each other. They challenge each other. They fight with everything they've got. They use weapons. They use their special skills. They use their powers.

They're not fighting for prizes. They're not fighting for honor. They're fighting for their lives. Victory is their only option.

Let the games begin!

MEDUSA

The Gorgons probably lived around Libya.
This is a country in northern Africa.

Medusa is a monster in Greek myths. She's one of the Gorgons. Gorgons are 3 sisters. Medusa is the protector. The other 2 sisters are Stheno and Euryale. Stheno means "strong." Euryale means "wise."

The Gorgons have scaly bodies. They have round faces. They have flat noses. They have tongues that flop out of their mouths. They have large teeth that stick out. They have sharp claws. They have wings. They have snakes for hair. The snakes are **venomous**. Venom is poison that is injected by biting. The venom can kill in minutes. The snakes' tongues are always moving. They're always trying to bite down. The Gorgons' blood is also poisonous.

Gorgons are really ugly. Their **gaze** is deadly. Gaze is a look or stare. When people look at them, they turn to stone. The Gorgons turned sailors into rocks and reefs. They turned giants into mountains.

Medusa is the only **mortal** Gorgon. Mortal means not being able to live forever. Medusa ages like humans. Her sisters were born as monsters. But Medusa was born as a beautiful human. She had long, flowing blonde hair. The god of the sea fell in love with her. This made Athena mad. Athena is the goddess of wisdom and war. She turned Medusa's hair into snakes. She made Medusa's face ugly. She made her more scary than her sisters.

Athena also turned Medusa's skin green.

Perseus is a Greek hero. He cut off Medusa's head. He had to trick her. He didn't look at her. He used a shiny shield. The shield acted like a mirror. This is how he was able to cut off her head. Her blood spilled into seaweed. This became the rocks in the Red Sea.

FUN FACTS ABOUT MEDUSA

- Medusa was punished. She was sent to Africa. She wandered around in Africa. Some baby snakes fell from her head. The snakes stayed in Africa. They grew and had babies. People believe this is why there are so many snakes in Africa.

- Sicily is a large island. It's in the Mediterranean Sea. It's off the coast of Italy. Medusa is on the flag of Sicily. Instead of snakes, she has wheat for hair.

- Medusa also has another set of 3 sisters. They are called the Graeae. Their names are Deino, Enyo, and Pemphredo. They shared 1 eye and 1 tooth.

HEL

Norse gods called the underworld Helheim.
This means "Hel's home."

Hel is a **Norse** goddess. Norse means coming from the Norway area. Hel is a goddess of the dead. She rules the **underworld**. The underworld is a place where dead souls live. It's where people go when they die. It's also called hell. It is cold and dark.

Hel is the only female goddess with her own world. She rules over people who die without glory. She rules over people who died from sickness. She rules over people who died from old age. She rules over people who did crimes.

Hel is a monster. Half her body is alive. Half her body is dead. Her living half is pretty. Her dead half is ugly. Her bones are outside her body. Her skin is rotting. Hel smells like a dead person.

Both of Hel's parents are giants. Hel's father is Loki. Loki is a **trickster** god. Tricksters play jokes on others. Hel's mother is Angrboda. Hel's brothers are a giant snake and a wolf. They're monsters. They were born in a dark cave. The gods were scared of them. They knew they'd bring doom. So, the gods kicked them out. That's how Hel ended up in Helheim.

Hel's name means "hidden." The dead are hidden from the living.

Hel decides where to send each dead soul. Helheim has different places for different souls. She sends killers and robbers to a shore of **corpses**. Corpses are dead bodies. She also sends them to a cave filled with snakes. Snake poison drips down the walls.

The road to Helheim is rough. It's called Hellway. There's a river. It's the border between life and death. It's freezing cold. It has knives floating in it. The only way to cross the river is over the bridge. Dead souls have to pay to cross. They pay with their blood.

FUN FACTS ABOUT HEL

- Hel has a special ship. The ship is called Naglfar. It's made from the fingernails and toenails of the dead. Norse people have a tradition. They trim dead people's hair and nails. They do this before burying them. They don't want their nails to be included in Naglfar.

- The Norse people see Hel as dangerous. The Dutch and Germans see her in a nicer way. They see her as "Frau Holle." Frau means "married woman" or "mother." Frau Holle is the goddess of death and renewal. She's an old woman. She lives in a world at the bottom of a well.

- In Danish stories, a helhest is a horse with 3 legs. It's connected with death and sickness. Hel rides on the helhest. She does this while killing men.

CHOOSE YOUR BATTLEGROUND

Medusa and Hel are fierce fighters. They're well-matched. They're both scary. But they have different ways of fighting. They have different strengths and weaknesses. So, choose your battleground carefully!

Battleground #1: Sea

• Medusa would fight well in the sea. She comes from the sea. She lives on an island. Her family members are sea gods or sea monsters.

• Hel lives in the underworld. But her castle is by a river.

Medusa is featured in a lot of artwork.

Battleground #2: Land

- Medusa could also fight on land. She'd prefer the daytime. People won't be able to see her at night. This means she can't turn them to stone. She also won't be able to see as well at night.

- Hel could fight in the day. But she'd prefer the nighttime. She lives in the dark. She lives under the ground. She's not used to the sunlight.

Battleground #3: Mountains

- Medusa has made most of the rocks and mountains. She'd be fine moving around them.

- Hel's underworld is like a big, dark cave. Mountains have a lot of caves.

ARMED AND DANGEROUS: WEAPONS

Medusa: Medusa's head is her best weapon. After Perseus cut off Medusa's head, he put it on a stick. He used it as a weapon. He gave Medusa's head to Athena. Athena placed Medusa's head on her shield. Her head was still deadly.

Hel: Hel's best weapon is a dog named Garm. Garm is a hellhound. Hellhounds are dogs of hell. Garm guards Hel's gates. Its teeth are stained with blood. Its fur is stained with blood. It howls wildly. It howls at the start of wars. It lives in a dark cave. It kills. It can only be calmed by hel-cakes. These are special breads from hell.

FIGHT ON!

The battle begins! It's early evening. The sun has set. It's almost nighttime. But it's still light out. Medusa sails in from her island. Hel emerges from Helheim. Medusa and Hel are going to fight on land. They're in a forest. There are trees all around them.

Move 1:

Hel closes her eyes. She breathes deeply. She calms herself. She focuses on her sense of hearing. She listens for Medusa's snakes. Medusa has a lot of snakes on her head. She can be heard for miles. Snakes make hissing sounds. They rattle. They rub their scales together. This makes dry, scratchy sounds.

Helheim is 1 of 9 worlds in Norse mythology.

Move 2:

Medusa looks for Hel. Sometimes, she has to move the snakes out of her eyes. It's almost dark. Hel blends in with the night. Medusa has to look carefully. She finally sees Hel. She slowly walks toward her. She wants to surprise her.

Move 3:

Hel hears Medusa coming. The snake sounds get louder. Hel is like other **Vikings**. Vikings are Norse warriors. Hel knows how to use swords. She knows how to fight in battles. She takes out her sword. She slashes at Medusa's head. She misses, but chops off some of her snakes.

Medusa's parents are Phorcys and Ceto.
All their children are monsters.

LIFE SOURCE: FOOD FOR BATTLE

Medusa: Medusa is mortal. That means she eats things that humans would eat. Since she turns living things to stone, she probably eats vegetables. Vegetables aren't living things. So, they wouldn't turn to stone. Medusa would be able to eat them. The snakes in Medusa's hair probably eat things normal snakes eat. Snakes eat live prey like mice.

Hel: Hel lives in a big castle. It's named Eljudnir. This means "damp with sleet." Sleet is frozen rain. The outside walls are icy. Everything in her house has a name. Her knife is "starvation." Her plate is "famine." Her table is "hunger." Hel has apple orchards around her castle. Eating Hel's apples causes strange dreams. In some stories, Hel eats dead flowers and blood.

Move 4:

The cut snakes hit the ground. They're still moving. They don't die right away. They're alive for a little bit. They **slither** toward Hel. Slither means to move in a twisting motion.

Move 5:

Hel opens her eyes. But she looks down. She remembers not to look at Medusa. She stomps on the snake heads. She keeps doing this. She kills the snakes. Meanwhile, the snakes on Medusa's head grow back.

Move 6:

Medusa knows her blood is deadly. She gets some darts. She dips them in her poisonous blood. She plans on throwing the darts at Hel.

Hela is the Marvel Comics character based on Hel.

AND THE VICTOR IS . . .

What are their next moves?

Who do you think would win?

Medusa could win if:

- She covers her nose. Hel smells really bad. Half her body is rotting away. Hel's smell could distract Medusa. It would burn her eyes.

- She catches Hel off guard. Hel just has to look at her once to turn to stone.

Hel could win if:

- She learns to fight without looking at Medusa. She could practice fighting **blindfolded**. Blindfolded means having a piece of cloth covering the eyes.
- She takes an **antidote** for snake venom. Antidotes are medicine. They cancel out venom and poison. They cure and heal.

Both Hel and Medusa are female monsters in ancient myths.

Medusa: Top Champion

Ladon was Medusa's brother. He was a dragon. His body was shaped like a snake. He had 100 heads. He didn't need to sleep. He lived in the Garden of Hesperides. This garden was at the farthest west corner of the world. It was at the edge of the ocean. The garden had many special things. But the most important thing was the tree that made golden apples. Golden apples made the gods and goddesses **immortal**. That means anyone who ate them would live forever. They would never be hungry or thirsty or sick. Ladon guarded the golden apples. He made sure no one but the gods could eat the golden apples.

Hel: Top Champion

Fenrir was Hel's brother. He was a giant wolf. He never stopped growing. He kept getting bigger and bigger. His drool formed rivers. His jaws reached from the ground to the sky. The gods were scared of him. They tried to chain him. But he kept breaking chains. The gods had dwarfs make magical chains. They tricked Fenrir. They bound him to a large rock with the magical chains. This made Fenrir mad. Fenrir became the gods' enemy. He dreamed of revenge. His heart was filled with hate and rage. He was trapped for many years. He was trapped until Ragnarok. Ragnarok was a big war that caused the doom of the gods. Fenrir got loose. He ran around. He ate everything in his way. He had 2 sons. His 2 sons were also giant wolves. One son swallowed the sun. The other son swallowed the moon.

Consider This!

THINK ABOUT IT!

- How are Medusa and Hel alike? How are they different? Are they more alike or different? Why do you think so?
- Would you rather fight Medusa or Hel? Explain your answer.
- What skills do you have to fight Medusa? What skills do you have to fight Hel?
- What is Medusa's role in Greek myths? What is Hel's role in Norse myths?
- Read the 45th Parallel Press book about Hel. What more did you learn about her?

LEARN MORE!

- Hoena, B. A. *Medusa and Her Oh-So-Stinky Snakes.* North Mankato, MN: Stone Arch Books, 2020.
- Loh-Hagan, Virginia. *Hel.* Ann Arbor, MI: Cherry Lake Publishing, 2018.
- Nagle, Frances. *Medusa.* New York, NY: Gareth Stevens Publishing, 2017.
- Napoli, Donna Jo, and Christina Balit (illustr.). *Treasury of Norse Mythology: Stories of Intrigue, Trickery, Love, and Revenge.* Washington, DC: National Geographic, 2015.

GLOSSARY

antidote (AN-tih-dote) medicine that cures or cancels out venom or poison

blindfolded (BLINDE-fohld-ed) to have something covering one's eyes so one can't see

corpses (KORPS-iz) dead bodies

gaze (GAYZ) the stare or intense look someone gives you

immortal (ih-MOR-tuhl) being able to live forever

mortal (MOR-tuhl) a living thing that can die

Norse (NORS) coming from the Norway area

opponents (uh-POH-nuhnts) fighters who compete against each other

slither (SLITH-ur) to move in a twisting motion

trickster (TRIK-stur) someone who likes to play tricks

underworld (UHN-dur-wurld) a place where dead souls live

venomous (VEN-uhm-uhs) having poison that is injected by biting

victor (VIK-tur) the winner

Vikings (VYE-kingz) Norse warriors

warriors (WOR-ee-urz) fighters

INDEX